This book is dedicated to my beloved,
late husband Roy Harsh,
and to Colin, Kisuri and Michael

Twelve and Three Quarter Steps

To a Life of Wealth,

Prosperity,

and Joy

Published by Argyll-River LLC

ISBN 978-0-9897705-0-7

Editor: Gloria Campbell
Cover Designer: Connie De La Vergne

Printed in the United States of America

Table of Contents

Introduction

You were born with wings,
why prefer to crawl through life.
Rumi

Everything in the universe is within you.
Ask all of yourself.
Rumi

I believe that our highest purpose in life is to live in total joy. The Source which expresses Itself as each of us intended that our experience of human-hood should be totally fulfilling in all areas of life so that you and I could mirror in our lives the qualities of the Super Being who lives in, as, and through each one of us. How do we live in wealth, and how do we do it in joy, and what is true prosperity?

In my mind, they are synonymous terms, but I will define each so that the points made further on may have greater clarity.

Webster says wealth is "Large possessions and resources, and all objects which have value to many." I have to admit that when I read this some years back, it looked daunting, if not impossible; I could not imagine large numbers of possessions and resources, and the concept of largess was very far away. I had a great many changes before me, and the biggest ones were drastic alterations in my thinking.

Of prosperity, the dictionary simply states: "Success and economic wellbeing," and prosperity as "a state of economic thriving." I would posit that prosperity is far more than abundant money and resources; it is a condition which touches every part of our lives, not just economics, but love, inner peace, beautiful relationships, health, success, and contentment and general well-being.

Webster says joy is "a sense of well-being." For me, joy is the underpinning of everything. Without joy, life is hardly worth the effort—in fact, it is drudgery. Joy is the essence of the Spirit which expresses as each of us. The more we recognize that we are sustained by that Presence, the more joy wells up within us; we become more aware that there's nothing to get upset about because The Essence resolves every issue.

We all want to be happy and healthy and comfortable and live fulfilling lives. I have had my own rather speckled journey and have learned a few things along the way as I have progressed into a very comfortable space. This book is about sharing with you the methods I have used. There was no silver spoon for me. The way through and out took study and perseverance and a willingness to change my thinking. It's quite simple which doesn't necessarily mean easy. But change can occur in your life, just as it did for me, and I will state that again and again, a little differently each time. You will find that the words "mind bending" will occur regularly as you read on and that is by design. To achieve a different quality of life you will need to change your mind, and you will find that you can do it. The payoff is enormous and well worth the effort.

It is my intention to lead you along a series of steps, each building on the last but all inter-related to a point where you will be aware all the time of what to think and how, and find yourself progressing toward a different life. Whatever your starting point now, you can get there from here. Life wasn't meant to be hard; it was meant to be fun! Illness, poverty, hardship, and misery were not, and are not, part of the plan; a life of inner contentment can be yours too, and you will arrive at these by changing your thinking.

All Wealth Arises From Within

From earliest times, great sages have taught that all people can have their abundant good without in any way taking it from others or preventing others from getting what they also want. These ideas have been lost or buried for much of our history, or kept in the hands of a select few who benefitted from that non-disclosure. But now this knowledge is available to all who want it. Everyone, everyone has the power within to be self-sufficient and happy, and it is with this thought in mind that I offer a way for you to get there, and unless I had done it for myself, I would not have the courage to suggest it. This book is not a collection of money-making tips, and, in most cases, it will not fix your troubles overnight (although it can if you are truly aware). It is not a book you can read once and add to the bookshelf, and it is certainly not the last word on the subject. It is a way forward if you care to achieve freedom. It is a series of motivating signposts. It is the way that I have proven for myself, and it is with the desire to assist you that I offer it.

Once again, please remember the phrase "mind bending" as you read on because no permanent behavioral change will occur without the restructuring of your out-worn modes of processing information. Some of us, for instance, have the misconception that all we want in life is "out there" for us to take hold of before someone else beats us to it or cheats us out of it. But, actually, unless you have an interior consciousness of *abundance*, there is little hope that it will come to you or stay with you.

This book is the result of my ongoing journey. It is a love story, and it is my gift and contribution to the happiness of all who can use it. Walk with me and arrive at that blissful place of loving life which came for me after years of depression and penury. Through the process of mental housecleaning, you can free yourself of destructive habits, and re-direct your new-found energy to the purpose of creating the fulfillment of your desires.

What seemingly comes to you is what you have generated and attracted through your own realization of the overflowing Source within you. You have come to the earth-plain with all the inner equipment you need to live a prosperous and happy life, but do you understand yourself well enough to use that equipment?

Chapter One
Accept—Open a Channel

Be still and know that I am God.
Psalm 46:10

Everything that you can ever want or expect to achieve in this life is first created within the mind and then infused with loving emotion to bring it into material form. Within each of us is that spark of Life for which we have many names. Some call it God, others prefer Spirit, yet others refer to The Power, Energy, or Source. Whatever you call it, it is in the awareness of your union with this inner something that desires are initiated and dreams are made manifest.

But how can this be done? How do you access this Inner Being so that the wishes you have may become your reality and show up in your material experience?

One place to begin is with the cultivation of mental stillness, for it is in a quiet mind where conscious thought is diminished, that Spirit can speak to you and you can

6

listen and respond. In the clatter of daily life with its multiple demands and unrelenting inner voices, it can be difficult to reach your Inner Self. So I invite you to begin this process: find a quiet place where you will not be disturbed—no iPhone, media, pets, or people, and release yourself and seek your Source and the root of your being.

Sit comfortably and just be in touch with *you*. Free yourself from the demands of your day and just be alone. Withdraw your attention from everything and relax. How do you do that? Just focus on your body. Feel its sensations, notice any pressure, and perhaps scan for aches or discomfort. Then take several deep breaths.

But wait. Stop! Don't rush this step. Gently exhale all the air that you can, then inhale to your capacity and do this several times in order to initiate the relaxation response. How do you feel now? How do your feet and hands feel, and your back? If any part of you aches, breathe deeply and direct the flow to that area. Focus on your head and let go of your usual expression. Let your jaw drop. Let your brow relax. Feel your way mentally down your back and shoulders, chest and arms with the intention of relaxing everything. Continue through all the parts of your body down to your feet and ask your body to just go limp.

This can be a scary experience for those of you who need continual noise and agitation in order to feel okay.

There may be a sense of being out of control and frighteningly alone. Until I was in my mid-forties, I felt that way and wondered whether there was "anyone home" in there. I found that I did not particularly want to revisit that emptiness too often, and sometimes it made me cry. But I stayed with the practice and gradually saw the discomfort fade and found myself longing to get back to the stillness of that silent place. What I gradually realized, with patience and persistence, was that during that meditation time many of my problems and concerns were being clarified and solved, whether it was how to build a fence, or plan a menu, or relate to a troubling person. This was a wonderful payoff and it kept my interest.

So, now that you have relaxed your body, begin to pay attention to your breathing. This is very simple. Just focus on the underside of your nose—it may tingle and actually assist concentration—and be conscious of your intake and exhalation. This process will calm you quicker than anything you can name because what is happening now is that the mind is beginning to quiet down, and that is the objective.

You are going to find that your mind does not want to cooperate. Don't worry, all meditators experience this and learn to gently return their attention to the breath again, and again, and again. Just be aware that the train of thoughts will continue to rush on and that your job is to keep your cool and concentrate on breathing.

Why are you going to all this trouble? So that in time, you, too, can experience the calmness which can open a channel to your own Spirit, and so your creative center will be tangible and available.

Remember that I said up front that you would encounter mind bending ideas throughout these pages? Well, we are up and running. Right now you are requiring your mind to modify its behavior away from the continual rampage of ungoverned thoughts to acceptance that it is a wonderful tool but is not in charge and does not run the show. The energies of the mind need to be harnessed to be of real use. As I have said, your mind will not respond with ecstatic delight. It will fight you all the way, and you will gently counter its resistance by meditating daily for about 15 minutes. Over time, you will reap the benefits by drawing to you the desires of your heart.

Are you still bucking the process or rushing on to the next chapter in the hope that you can evade this step? I understand. Change isn't easy. The rampant mind likes having control and keeping you stuck.

"Isn't there an easier way?" I hear you say. "I haven't time; my day is stretched to the max already." To which I can only respond that in the long run this *is* the easy way.

Years ago when I was starting to get interested in the value of mind control, I tried to ignore this process—and simply lost time and started over again and again. Now I appreciate its purpose. It restored me to myself—my True Self. Meditation focuses my energy and intention. It brings inner peace. It centers my creative energies. It refreshes body and spirit. It makes clear to me every day what I am *really* about in this lifetime and, invariably, there is a message which comes through as a suggested next step.

If any of those benefits appeal to you, pause before you read on and begin the rest of your life. The common belief is that you have to scurry around frantically and do everything yourself because you think it all depends on you. It doesn't. Take the short-cut. Recognize now that one way to achieve anything is to discover your Source and let It create your desired good with you and through you and for you.

Footnote: In their book *Finding the Path to Joy through Energy Balance*, Esther and Jerry Hicks speak of "turning it over to The Manager." There's wonderful support for you here.

Chapter Two
Choose

*Not choice, but habit rules
the unreflecting herd.*
William Wordsworth

Choice is a transcending capacity, and an innate gift, because it's part of your power to achieve, to become, and to manifest absolutely anything which you can hold in your mind.

Stop for a moment and think about those words. GET their magnitude! It is not outside influences; it is not other people; it is not your upbringing; it is not luck or lack of it, and it certainly isn't chance.

When you *choose*, you are thinking, and the masters of all ages agree that therein rests our magnificence. It is through thought that you have the power to change yourself and your life. As Charles Hannel says in his book *The Master Key,* "Thoughts are the connecting link between the Infinite and the finite, between the Universal and the individual."

The Conscious Mind Thinks and the Subconscious Mind Acts

So how does all this come about? It's fairly simple in theory, but quite challenging in practice and it *will* take practice! Your conscious mind thinks a thought, and your subconscious mind listens and delivers. What could be simpler than that? So if you think "I don't have enough money," your subconscious hears you and will act upon your thought, and you won't have enough money. If you think "I am over weight," you're right. The weight will stay with you. Multiply that by umpteen repetitions, as we humans are prone to do, and you will find it a perpetual condition until you change the thought.

How does this work? Pared down to its basic elements, it's like this: the mind has two phases of operation. The conscious mind thinks and chooses. (That's you and me every day, thinking about whatever we think and plan.) The other part or function of the mind is the subconscious, which does not think or choose—it simply *does*—acts on whatever the conscious mind thinks about. The subconscious doesn't ask questions. It doesn't make evaluations. It simply carries out to the letter what the conscious mind has decided to think about. In his decisive book, *Beyond Positive Thinking,* Dr. Robert Anthony puts it this way: "Your subconscious mind cannot decide . . . it must be told what to do, it cannot, will not think for itself, so we, our conscious selves, must be responsible for our choices."

So, if you decide to think: "My husband is a jerk," or "My wife's not pulling her weight," or "My boss is a pain," or "I can never seem to get ahead,"

Or you think: "I am having a wonderful day," or "My children always do well in school," or "I live an abundant and healthy life," or "I am loving and I am loved," then you are right in both cases because your subconscious mind will deliver to you in your outward life whatever you choose to hold in your mind. When you are thinking, you are choosing and that choice is created by your subconscious in your material experience.

With *every* thought you send a message to your subconscious mind. This is as true of your positive pronouncements as it is of the unrecognized, unexamined, habitual patterns of your thinking which have probably been with you for years. *All* of it is creative material for the subconscious, and *all* of it shows up for you in your physical life.

Be Careful What You Think Because You Are Creating It

So let's say that you want a larger house, a better job, or a compatible life partner. You *can* have anything you want. Part of the trick to getting it is to be very specific in your thinking. For instance what year, make, model, and color of car? What mileage, interior, history, and extras do you want?

The same process is true for the house. What style, square footage, location, price range, amenities, school district, and view? As you think about these items you are making choices.

If it's a loving companion you're thinking about, form an image in your mind. Think about the qualities you want that person to have, the interests, and capabilities of the desired mate. All of these inner reflections on your part are sending a message to your subconscious so that they may appear in your outward life. You might make a note of the words of Dr. Wayne Dyer, "Whatever you give your attention to grows."

I have found two wonderful homes by this means, and in the course of writing this material, I attracted my third and now the fourth is in process of creation. The most extraordinary and beloved partner came to me this way, and I went from rickety health to restoration and strength by this very power of thought.

Three Important Points

The first is about the time frame for the fulfillment of your desires. Make your choice and outline all the details with the understanding that the good you claim will come to you at exactly the right time for your life journey and spiritual progress. You don't get to tell the Spirit how to do it or when. You do not know the over-all plan for your life. The Spirit of you does; besides, putting a time frame on the fulfillment of a desire may prevent it from showing up at the earliest possible date. So leave it alone *knowing* that it will appear when the time is right. And, as you are making your choice, say, "This or something better." This leaves your Source free to answer in ways which may astonish you and deliver far more than you could have dreamed of.

I have experienced this many times, most notably when buying a house I loved. The deal fell through, but the next option far exceeded my delight in the first. My daughter had a similar experience with a job search; several desirable options appeared and went away but because she was able to say, "This or something better in Your perfect time," the most advantageous place became available to her.

The second point concerns the wanting of your perfect mate: You can't decide for someone else. You can't set your sights on Sally Marvel or Peter Wonder and claim that she or he is unequivocally yours and will somehow take the bait. No. All you have to do is decide that the best and most awesome person in all of creation is being drawn to you, and, after all, you really don't care who it is so long as they are wonderful for you.

Third, once you have chosen your desired good and spoken your words, you're done! Let it be. Your Inner Self will take over and all you have to do is be open and allow things to unroll. No worries. No "What ifs." No agitation. Let go and allow . . . .

You Are Always Choosing

Now comes the tricky part. Having once made your desires known and set your power of creation to work, will you consistently support that? Or will you fall prey to statements which contradict and negate?

If, having made your choices clear, you meet with a friend and complain: "I can't afford a new car," look what has happened. You just made another choice—totally inconsistent with what you said you wanted. Do you see the subtlety of this? We are always choosing! And your subconscious mind will pick this up, and you have cancelled your dream.

Or suppose that you have found that lovely house and affirm that it's yours, then chat with your friend on the phone and tell him, "it's way beyond my means." Bingo! You've created a doubt which will impede your taking possession of the good you earlier claimed.

Perhaps in your quiet meditation when the channel was open, you conceived of a beautiful man or woman walking into your life and being with you and made that a definite choice. Then you say to a friend, "All the possible best partners are taken."

I told you it was simple, but challenging. Here we run into another mind bender. If you really want what you want, you will have to monitor your thoughts and weed out the contradictions, assiduously and continually. *Yes,* you can. Many of us have. I have. It takes practice, and then more practice.

Please don't gloss over this lightly. Make your choice and be with the process—you will succeed, and you will find in time that sometimes you'll get a little more joy and delight than you bargained for and will open your heart to bigger possibilities and stretch your inner growth. It has happened to me.

I had recently ended a long marriage quite late in life. What did I want now? I thought about the joy of falling in love again, since I had not experienced that for 30 years, and so I made my choice and let it go with the certainty that it would come about. Not too long after, I told my Inner Mind, through thought, that I wanted a companion to take me to the opera, symphony, and ballet since I did not drive at night. I got on with what was immediate and left the work to my subconscious mind which I equate with The Source of my being.

Sometime later I "chanced" to run into a man with whom I had been acquainted over many years. I thought nothing of it—at first—but after coffee and several lunches, I was deeply in love. The surprise was that he was passionate about opera and ballet and, of course, wanted to take me with him! I had not thought that both of my desires might come in one package.

I related to you that I was in love, but he was not (or so it seemed at the time). Do I need to draw pictures of the ecstasy and agony of that? He was wonderful company; he was the most evolved person I had ever met; he loved everyone unconditionally; and he really enjoyed being with me, but that one little important part was missing: he did not have for me the personal love which I felt for him. So for all that I had accomplished and drawn into my space, I felt that the scenario was incomplete and I was hurting. So I took my questions and longings into meditation and asked my Spirit what I had to learn here.

What I came to realize was that this jewel of a being, whom everyone loved and who touched all hearts with gentleness and made them feel so good about themselves, was with me to teach me how to appreciate myself and learn to love unconditionally which I had never done before. My association with him also brought me to the realization that I had some forgiving to do of several people in my life, and that I could not move forward, or truly love him, until that was done. So I wrote to all of them. Forgave them all, sent them gifts, and found a new inner peace. Talk about getting more than you bargained for!

But perhaps the most profound gift of all was that I who had asked to fall in love had not specified that the feeling be mutual! I had not stated that I wanted the one I loved to fall in love with me. So I went back to the drawing board. I claimed devoted, mutual, enduring love with a man with whom I would be compatible, and if it were not too be this superman, some other would come into my space and fulfill that longing: "This or something better in Your own perfect time." This was my letting go.

I shall revisit this story a little later. I still had so much to learn, and my path may have value for you.

So let's go back to *your* choices for a moment and consider some ways to support your consistency of thought and accomplishment of *your* dreams. Write your creative thought down and carry it with you and refer to it often. Place an image of the wanted item where you will often see it. Put yourself (mentally) in the driver's seat of the car and feel the feelings, and test drive it, and then feel the exhilaration. Creating a scrapbook of pictures of the things you want also fixes your choices on your mind. Live with and in the reality of what you want; the more you feel it and love it the quicker it will show up in your world.

Embrace the mind bender of making a choice and refusing to cancel it, or letting anyone tell you it can't be done. Rather than risk the negatives that others will sometimes offer, just don't tell them until you have realized your intention. This practice calls for discipline— and you have it, and the payoff is worth it, because it is a tool for getting everything you want.

Please hear Joseph Murphy's enlightened words: "If you think 'poverty' thoughts you will become poor no matter how rich you are now. If you make a habit of thinking of riches, spiritual and mental, you must become rich according to the law of reciprocal relationship. In other words when you think 'wealth is mine now,' and remain faithful to that idea your subconscious mind will respond by distributing wealth along all lines according to the nature of your thought life" (from *Your Infinite Power to be Rich*).

Chapter Three

Deserve

*Whatever self-image we have accepted
puts a ceiling on the use of our potential.
Beyond Positive Thinking,*
Dr. Robert B. Anthony

Do you really feel that you deserve all the wonderful
things that you want in your life? Do you really feel at the
deepest level of your being that you are worthy and that
your dreams can be realized, and that you can bring them
into reality?

Many people don't believe that on a subconscious
level. Some strive for years to accomplish their goals,
perhaps with limited success and self-sabotage because of
erroneous beliefs nested in the subconscious which
militate against their best efforts.

The simple truth is that *yes,* you are absolutely
deserving of all the happiness, wealth, joy, and love that the
Universe has always destined and intended for you to
receive. As Esther and Jerry Hicks say in *"Ask and It is Given,"*

Part 2, (*The Law of Attraction*) "You were created to experience outrageous joy."

What you want is *always* available for you. The glitch is that many of us limit or refuse the things we ask for, due to unexamined barriers and ground-in beliefs which can prevent us from allowing and accepting the good we consciously choose. Many, probably most, of these obstacles were implanted when we were impressionable children and bred into us for the sake of conformity and acceptable behavior.

I certainly wasn't immune to this process. How often, for instance, did I hear my mother say, "Stop wanting things and think about what you can do without," and, "We can't afford it." Or "Stop looking at those who have more, and think of those who have less." Bless her heart—she did the best she knew, but I grew up feeling wrong, greedy, undeserving, and voiceless, worth little, and worthy of little. I had the lowest expectations and no tools to create a prosperous life or do better than my parents had done. How could such repeated comments foster a desire to grow and expand, let alone feel good about it? The residue of that conditioning took me years to understand and many more to reprogram.

I was in my thirties when my then husband and I moved into a modest house on a very sparse income and because I had no discretionary money, I made a dress out of worn-out, old curtains the former owners had left behind! I shudder to admit it but do so only because it was a turning point, a signal that I had to change my appreciation of myself. Some years later and with young children and still in a state of relative penury, I would joke to people, "We are living on the edge of extinction," until one day I really heard—with shock—what I was saying and knew again that I had to work on my self-concept. So I upgraded to: "We always have enough." Much later I was able to refine that further and state, "We always have more than we need." As if those were not examples enough, very much later in life as I was trying to repair a leak in a ceiling while my then husband sat and watched, it hit me again. "Your self-worth is still in the toilet." "What are you going to do?" I asked myself.

I left the situation and that life behind and began to work assiduously on my feelings of self-worth.

I read books on self-esteem. I used nearly continuous affirmative statements to shore up new beliefs and cancel the habitual negative messages. I studied people who were successful and sought to associate with them as often as possible. I started window shopping and claiming lovely things in my future experience, and I imagined how I would feel and act as a wealthy and opulent person and made strides in that direction.

This is part of my story—but what of yours? Did your folks scrimp and buy the cheapest–and justify it somehow? Did they say, "Do you think I'm made of money?" Or "Make do with what you've got"? And what about such phrases as "The rich hog it all," and "The rich take it from the poor"? Such comments and attitudes lodged in your absorbent child-mind may have translated as "I'm not worthy," and "I don't count for much," and "I don't deserve it." Did they also say that, "Money is hard to come by," and "Life was meant to be tough and build character," and "You have to work hard for whatever you get"? Life isn't meant to be tough, and you have all the character you'll ever need.

These erroneous messages need to be understood for what they are—false information often delivered by good, well-meaning people who didn't know any better and learned it from those who were equally ignorant. You certainly can come to a point where you recognize what has happened to you, and, that done, you can empower yourself to override false information, replace it with newly learned convictions of self-worth and worthiness, and rebuild your self-concept and your life.

Did I say something earlier about mind benders? Well, you just met another one! There's work to be done here for those willing to change their thinking so that they can accomplish their dreams. So let's look at some beliefs which are lodged within and prevent your gaining what you desire.

The belief that you can't really change will trip you consistently, and it simply isn't true. That's a good one to get rid of. Simply reprogram that to "I am capable of achieving anything I set my mind to." Or you can repeat to yourself frequently, "I have within me all the power and energy that I need to accomplish my intentions."

The belief that the rich have it all and hog it and resenting them will keep all good at a distance. In my belief, you are one with your Source. Your wealth is not dependent upon nor does it come from anywhere or anything else. It is the product of your knowing that it is your right to be happy and wealthy.

"Nobody in my family has ever amounted to much." Maybe that's so, but it doesn't have to apply to you. You create your life plan. You follow your dreams, and if you will open your thinking and change your mind, you *can* have what you choose.

"Life is hard." Saying that is not going to help at all. Drop it. Never utter that phrase again. Say to yourself often, "My life is beautiful," and say with Bernie Siegel, "I see beauty in all things everywhere."

It's all in your attitude, and you can change that.

The belief that "I wasn't supposed to have much" is quite useless, not to say untrue. You can alter that to "I and my Source are one, and I lack nothing."

"My parents were really hard workers, and they didn't get rich." That may be so, but you have new information, abilities, and talent, and you can excel if you will believe that you can. Besides, here's another mind bender—you don't have to work hard to be wealthy! It is the quality of your consciousness which creates your wealth. And, quite without contradiction let me say, you may want to work hard at making money, but that's a choice. You can also cultivate the attitude that "Money comes to me easily and effortlessly." Thank you, Bob Proctor and Michelle Blood, and your book, *Be a Magnet to Money*.

An attitude of "Soak the rich" is fairly common among those who have a poverty self-concept. It is a worn-out idea.

Let it go. It simply points to ignorance of who you really are. You are a total unity with your Spirit, the infinite Source of you. Say to yourself, "I deserve to have everything I want and I accept it *now*."

By taking what belongs to others because "They can afford it and I haven't got much," you are telling yourself that you can't afford what they have. That's why you haven't got what they have. Plug in to that Spirit in meditation and believe and know that you are always provided for plentifully and, "I lack nothing that I want." As long as you take from others, you will block the flow of your good to you.

How can you change these inner patterns? Start by being aware of your thoughts and negative patterns, then cancelling and immediately replacing them with positive statements. Also, you will want to watch what other people say about their limitations—not to emulate—not to comment or criticize—but to learn and deepen your awareness.

Affirm the good you want often: "I have ever increasing income," or "I'm loving my new house." Always make your affirmative statements in the present tense— more on that later.

Work on your own self-esteem. Love *you*. Start replacing the endless interior negatives with only positive output. Says Jack Addington, author of *15 Keys to Prosperity,* "One who does not feel worthy of wealth cannot attract it."

As I worked on the changes I needed to make—and I, too, had a long road to travel in order to realize my own worth and potential—I noticed my life changing along the route with money appearing regularly, my housing getting better; even the friends I was attracting were wealthier and more aware.

I spoke in the last segment of a wonderful man whom I had met by requesting his presence from the Universal Being, but who seemed initially not to entertain a personal love for me. Within a week of my re-evaluating my asking, knowing, accepting, and expecting the arrival of my desires from The Source, Roy declared his love for me and to me and to the vast world of his friends! I, in turn, saw in him the expression of Source Itself manifesting for my joy.

The reason I incorporate this part of the story at this point in this work is because, it points to the progress I had made along my path of self-esteem. To draw into my world the loveliest man possible indicates that I had come to a point where I felt deserving of something better. He sensed my work in this area, and related having travelled a similar road earlier in life. He was generous in his praise, encouragement, and appreciation for me, and told me constantly how deserving I was of every possible good.

Life is a journey someone has said, and for most of us it often seems that it's uphill much of the time. It doesn't have to be. It was meant to be a joyful exploration. We shall always be learning, and how we see ourselves is pivotal. Sometimes, I still have rough days. Recently, as I groped my way out of such a phase, the words came into my mind, "If only you would remember *who* you are!"

Take heart. No matter where you are, you can get there from here. This is the starting point, and we all have to begin from where we are.

And please, as you go through your process, would you cut a corner which I did not know about during the earlier years of my journey? Would you keep in mind that when you incarnated onto this planet, you came whole and perfect, entire and without flaw. Your self-concept was untarnished. It has been the information to which you have been exposed and that you have picked up along the way that has caused you to doubt yourself. With that in mind, you may be able to make a quantum leap into wholeness—now.

This segment opened with a quote from Dr. R. Anthony which is hugely significant. You came in as pure potential—you still are. In the intervening years of your life, erroneous inputs to your thinking may have clouded that, but you can reclaim that pristine innocence, and know your True Self now—and act out of that realization.

Chapter Four

Speak

*Thou shalt decree a thing and it shall
be established unto thee.*
Job 22:28

We have spoken of the need to open a channel and create
a contact with our Inner Being. We have considered
making choices and how not to negate them. We have
looked at how self-concept can interfere with the
manifestation of the good we choose. Now let's examine
the power of speech and how we can best use that
wonderful gift.

This could be one of the shortest and most important
segments in the book. The whole message is that what you
speak is what you bring into your daily human experience.
What you say is what you get, or as Catherine Ponder puts it
in a leaflet published by Unity Church Worldwide, copyright
1976, "What you utter becomes your outer in your world."
Outside events do not make your reality, your thoughts
expressed as words do it—every time.

We have encountered a mind bender again. It's very similar to the one we discussed on the subject of thought patterns, but this time it will hit you right where you live—in your mouth. You think a thought and, in most cases, you rush out to vocalize it, and this is the time for vigilance and discipline, and a major question arises for consideration: If I say what's on my mind, how will it come back to me in material form?

"That woman is a bitch," you say, and that says nothing about her, but it reveals much about you, the speaker. We are a oneness, we creatures. We are part of the same Essence and what you do to, or say of, another comes back to knock on your door and disconnect you from your own essential feeling of well-being. If on the other hand, you say, "Namaste," which means "the God in me recognizes the God in you," then you have both been a blessing and raised the consciousness of the whole world. What you think and say does affect everyone.

Think of the negative things that people have called you in your life experience. Go on, just think of those for a minute. Do they make you feel good? Do you get a nice warm fuzzy from that? I suspect that your jaw tightens and your eyes narrow; you may even cringe a little and get a pain in your shoulders. The people who said those things may have been very well meaning, but you may have been hurt, and though such speakers had a momentary power trip, in the long run, they were diminished by their own words and attitude.

Now give your attention to the loving and encouraging words which have been spoken to you over the years. Feel them. Relish them. Re-live them. Your face softens and a smile may creep over it and a great expansiveness takes hold of your heart. Whoever delivered that balm to your soul created a well-being in you that stays. I will quote Dr. Robert Anthony again because his thinking is so pertinent: "Your word has power and if you will speak your word with conviction, your subconscious will act upon it without hesitation" (from *Beyond Positive Thinking*).

So, do you really want to live in joy and health and every kind of prosperity? Do you want to add to the fund of loving kindness in your world while at the same time growing by leaps and bounds into the exalted and sublime presence that you have the potential to be?

All You Have To Do Is Speak

I have found that when I really want something, and it is a "must have," speaking aloud is the most powerful way of getting my own attention. That's a funny way to put it, isn't it? "What do you mean," I hear you ask. "Aren't we addressing The Source now to deliver what we are asking for?"

Yes, we are speaking to The Source, and who do you think that is? It's you and me. It's that non-physical part of us which is our origin.

That little nubbin of wisdom aside, let's get back to the business of using words to achieve what you want.

As I said, when I am serious about a claim on the Spirit, I take a walk in the country, or a long drive, and I speak aloud. I outline the situation. I add in all the details, and I recognize the Power that I address while at the same time visualizing a perfect outcome and feeling the delight of that. I don't say what that outcome will look like; I just know that whatever it is, it will be just right. Having done that, I say "Thank you," and then I get on with whatever is next to do in my life. It works every time. I keep my mind on the fulfillment of my request or claim, and I do not worry it or in any way try to figure out how it can be done. That's not my business. My job is to live in gratitude and joy and the certain knowledge that what I have claimed is already a reality and will soon show up in my life.

There's another tool which I have used to great advantage and I want to share it here. There will be days when you just don't feel "up" and a grey gloom seems to lock you in, and if you are female, you'll probably just want to cry. I spent most of my first fifty years being depressed, and I developed some survival strategies. One of them was to acknowledge how I felt, and then to make brief, frequent statements to move me forward. "Things will get better," I told myself. "This won't last forever," was another. "This will pass," "I shall feel happy again," "I look forward to feeling good." Often this process was not awfully comforting, but it did set me up for better feelings after a while and did much to quell the nagging mind's efforts to keep me miserable and this is very important. I have mentioned before that your mind doesn't want to cooperate in these new moves you are making toward wholeness, so feeding it happy-making ideas limits its meddling.

Another ploy which I have used to great advantage is to simply speak positive, wonderful, and healing statements to myself almost continuously, particularly when I feel upset or I am struggling with something big. Years ago, at a time when I did not know which way to turn, I started repeating a statement again and again. "My life is blossoming into total perfection, "I said to myself. To begin with I didn't believe it. Why should I? I had no evidence to support such a claim. That, of course, is where faith comes in and that's another book, but it needs to be mentioned here because we sometimes have to walk through that "cloud of unknowing" before our experience changes. And change mine it did. Gradually, circumstances altered, avenues opened, the ways and means presented themselves, and I acted on them.

In view of that experience, and numerous others, I will suggest some statements with which you might start, and part of the reason for their inclusion is that they provide a way to keep the mind occupied on positive outcomes and helping you avoid worry so that The Source, or the subconscious, can fulfill your request without any negative input. The first is: "I feel wonderful." This was a statement Roy made continually in his last year of continual pain and discomfort. He never spoke of his many challenging conditions, even to his doctors, but practiced continual cheerfulness and gave everyone around him an example of living in utter joy. I hope the following will be useful to you.

"I love my life and it gets better all the time."
"I am filled with love, clarity, and peace."
"I see beauty everywhere I look."
"I am part of a happy and harmonious family."
"My sense of wellbeing grows stronger every day."
"I love and appreciate all the people who touch my life."
"The good I seek is seeking me."

"I give love to everything and everyone, and it comes back to me one hundredfold."

"Money flows to me and I always have plenty."

And this from E.V. Ingraham from *Wells of Abundance:* "I am filled with the Wisdom, love, power and Substance of God, and as an irresistible magnet, I draw to me all that is needful for my most complete expression of life." Using just this one statement as often as you wish will entirely change your consciousness, and thus change your life.

The list could go on and on, and you will create many statements which will make you feel good and bring that good right to your door. In thought and its expression in words lies one of your greatest tools and it has one more significant application.

In our culture we are of the understanding that it is essential to "Tell it as it is," to recount our stories, whether personal or national, with absolute clarity and keep them in the forefront of the mind so that "It can never happen again." This is erroneous thinking. It is the very reiteration of our sad stories and collective tragedies which keeps them alive and well and returning to us. Think again of the earlier explanation of the conscious and subconscious phases of the mind; the conscious thinks and the subconscious acts. As with thought, so with speech (which is just thought vocalized).

Carolyn Myss, in one of her many books, says, and I paraphrase, that when a painful event has happened in the life of a friend, we should listen to their story 3-4 times to allow them to vent and grieve. After that, any discourse on the subject needs to be deflected. "Let the dead bury their dead," and move on and think happy thoughts and speak happy words so that The Law of Attraction can "find" those vibes and return to the relief, happiness, contentment, and good times that you want.

I will close this segment with the words of Charles Barker, one of the most profound teachers, who said: "You always told God what you did not want, so you received more of it. You always receive what you declare, proving the power of the spoken word" (from *Treat Yourself to Life*).

Chapter Five

Want (For Others)

There is only One Self in all creatures. The one appears many,
just as the moon appears many reflected in water.
Mahatma Gandhi

This book is about getting what you want, and in order to get it, you have to be equally passionate about other people getting theirs and being absolutely and genuinely delighted that they do.

WOW! For many of us this is really troubling. Does that include my ex? Does that include the guy who took my job? Does that mean I have to be thrilled when my competitor does as well or better than I? Yeah, I know what you mean; it probably is as tough for you as it was for me.

Sometimes we are very competitive and feel that our efforts should result in greater gain than should the work of those who are less dedicated. Sometimes we think that people who don't have the work ethic that we have shouldn't do so well. Sometimes we feel that some people just have it all handed to them—the proverbial silver spoon—and never have to lift a finger. And then there are those whom we just don't like for one reason or another: "Why should they do better than I, and why should I care that they do as well or even better than I?"

So what are we to do? Perhaps recognizing where these attitudes come from would be a start. Think back over your life experience and what you have been taught. You have to work hard for a living. You have to take care of what you've got and make sure no one takes it. You have to make ends meet. You have to hold on to what you have and be frugal. You have to make your resources stretch. Money doesn't come easily. Why have *they* got more than we have? Make do. Mend your socks. Make your shirt last another season. The list goes on. And where does this pattern of limitation originate? Could it be from the feeling of having to defend one's self, and not run out and somehow have enough? Is it a pattern of poverty thinking which we have discussed before?

Then there's the dynamic side of us which feels that someone I don't like or who has wronged me should be punished and deserves to have a rough go of it, and why should I care? The "people make their own beds" sort of attitude. I have experienced this. I spent many years wishing that some people would get what I thought were their just desserts. I didn't prosper during that time, and those to whom I directed my wrath didn't seem any worse off while I felt they hung around my neck like the proverbial albatross.

Then Gandhi, Martin Luther King Jr., and so many others came along and jolted us into another reality. We have forgotten our origin and are out of alignment with whom we really are. We are *not* isolated little beings without a compass. We are one with Source Energy, with the soul of us, with that Spirit from whom we all are generated and who came with us to the planet and is always with us, expressing as us. We have forgotten that we are one with all other beings on Earth. We are one. We are part of that Only One without whom we could have no existence. Mahatma Gandhi has an appropriate word to say on this subject: "I am part and parcel of the whole, and I cannot find God apart from the rest of humanity."

This concept of Oneness is at once comforting, confusing, and scary—not to mention the responsibility it carries. It's a comfort because then we don't feel so alone and know that others like us are dealing with similar issues. It's confusing because we are all so individual and different and opposite, and somehow we have to blend and get along. And then scary because we are claiming oneness with some of the most strange, offbeat, and dangerous characters out there. As for responsibility, well think about it—we have to love them all because they are us! Wow! It always comes back to love—the biggest mandate and challenge and blessing of all.

So, if we are willing to accept that there is only One Life, One Mind, and One Source of everything that is, then you and I are part of that. We are the same thing, we are in it together, and all the good everyone wants is wanted by all of us and each has just as much right and is just as deserving as we are.

This brings us to a subject that is difficult, painful, and necessary—forgiveness. If we hate or dislike someone who has wronged us in some way, it's really distasteful to forgive, and nobody wants to do it. We feel justified in our position, and we feel that person is in the wrong.

So why should we forgive? I offer a couple of reasons: first, because we are all one and the same Spirit. We are all equally loved by our Source who wants the absolute best for each one, and Who appreciates each of Its individual creations with a passion which it is beyond our comprehension.

Second—and watch out here's another mind bender about to happen—all of those wrongs people aimed at us, all of the nasty words they said, and all the rotten things they did to make us unhappy, *they are not responsible for*. Yes. You did read that correctly. *They* are not responsible, and I do not mean that *they* should not be held accountable.

There is a law under which all creation operates, and it is called the Law of Attraction, and each of us uses this Law all the time whether we realize it or not. If we use it correctly by visualizing the best at all times, we derive great benefit, but if we misuse it by thinking of the negatives, we get into all sorts of pickles. Whatever has happened to you, you attracted it, and you are responsible. We shall go deeper into this in a coming segment, but for now, that much introduction is enough.

Now we can return to the subject of forgiving others for their (supposed) mistreatment of us with more understanding. There is in a sense nothing to forgive except *ourselves* for having drawn those events into our lives. The marvelous result of doing this inner work is that we free ourselves from the nagging, angry, and vengeful feelings we have held onto for so long and no longer need to feel disappointed, victimized, or trapped by the actions of another. Once you can achieve this freedom, it will seem quite natural to love everyone, to want the very best for them as you do for yourself. The quality of life changes then and the love you formerly withheld flows from you to all others and returns to you from everywhere. This idea is beautifully stated in *Getting into the Vortex* by Esther and Jerry Hicks: "When the success of another makes your heart sing, your resistance is gone and your own abundance soars."

One more thought about forgiving. There is another benefit over time. Angry thoughts and holding grudges will show up in your body down the road as a form of illness or disease.

If you want to be wealthy and prosperous and feel joyful, you have just discovered a big part of the recipe. You have travelled from a limiting meanness into an expansive attitude of all-inclusive love. In changing yourself to being one who treasures all others and in seeing only good in everyone, you have set in motion a pattern by which all good flows to you because what you give to others you give to yourself, and whatever you send out, will come back to you.

Chapter Six

See

Your life is the out-picturing of your inner pictures.
Joseph Murphy

The purpose of life is to be happy, and all the steps you are taking are designed to get you there as quickly as possible, so let's think about how *imaginative visualization* can move you forward. What I want to share with you has taken me the best part of a lifetime to learn and practice, so I'll make it as clear as possible so that you can take shortcuts.

To "see" means to visualize or to hold in the mind a picture of something you want to have appear in your outward life. It is the practice of encouraging the inward eye to rest on an object, a scene, a circumstance, or a situation the way you would like it to be or to unfold in your material experience. You could also so call it *pretending*! That's what you are doing—visually pretending that something *is* when it hasn't yet occurred. Of course, this involves believing and you might want to remember that the philosopher William James said, "Belief creates the actual fact."

It seems amazing that by simply imagining you can actually draw an event or object into your physical space. But why would you be surprised? You have already discovered what the power of thought can do, and the process of visualizing builds on that. Recall our discussion in Chapter Two about the conscious and the subconscious phases of the mind—how your conscious thinks thoughts and chooses what it wants and how the only role of the subconscious is to deliver the substance of what it thought about? The process of imagining is essentially the same, and holding an image in the mental visual field is like holding a thought in the mind except that now you are seeing pictures rather than just holding an idea, and perhaps you could contend that it's all the same thing. In any case, did Emerson have a point when he said, "You get what you think about most of the time"?

This is not a foreign idea, is it? Most of you see things in your heads all the time. The difference here is that when you visualize, you are doing it very deliberately and with a specific purpose in mind. You are using the imagination to create and steer the way your life will evolve and what you will invite into it. You are doing what Joseph Murphy speaks of when he says, "Your life is the out-picturing of your inner pictures."

Have you ever dashed into the grocery store first thing in the morning and said brightly to the clerk, "How's your day going?" Often to be told, "Okay so far." When I hear that response, I am inclined to think that I just met someone who's not consciously designing his or her day to be fabulous and abundant, which is really the only kind of day that most of us want. Personally, I don't like to take chances with my day. I like to get up in the morning and spell out the unrolling loveliness that I want with scenes and images in my mind. After all, says Mike Dooley with crisp brevity, "Thoughts become things."

When you decide to visualize, you are taking control. You are determining how things will be for you. Certainly you may not be able to sidestep an unexpected challenge or avoid troubling people, but by imagining your day as splendid, fulfilling, and happy, you are well on the way to feeling good no matter what turns up, and by feeling good, you are fulfilling the purpose of your life, not tomorrow or next week or at the weekend or when you're on vacation, but right now, in this moment, which is the only one you have.

By envisioning unexpected money coming to you or imagining the arrival of a surprise gift or seeing harmony in your relationships or feeling yourself whiz along the road in that yellow Lamborghini, you are deciding to live richly, rather than waiting to see what the day brings and whether you'll like it when it arrives. And, you may just want to push a little further and envision bigger changes. Consider what Dr. Robert B. Anthony has to say about the possibilities open to you: "The key to change is the ability to visualize a different situation, job, environment, car, or relationship" (*Beyond Positive Thinking*).

So let's get started. Perhaps you'll want to go into that quiet meditative state we spoke of in Chapter One. And having achieved inner calm, allow your mind to flow and you will quickly identify things you want. Pick one to start with and let your imagination bring it right to you. See the details, colors, shapes, size, even amount. Just rest with that for a while and relish the lovely feeling of *having* this thing you are creating.

Listen to that. *You* are creating it, that's how it works. As you envision what you have chosen in your mind, you are bringing it into being. Flesh it out to your heart's content, because as you continue to concentrate, other thoughts along those lines will come in too, and your dream is going to show up at some point in your life.

Will it be tomorrow? I don't know. Could be, but much will depend on how faithfully you keep that image in your mind and believe it to be yours *now*. I emphasize *now* because this item is yours *now*, not sometime in the amorphous future. Your thoughtful imagining has created this, and as you align your vibrations with it, it must emerge into your experience. Now remember, if you allow a negative idea entrance, you've just introduced another creation which you may not want so much.

You are an energetic, vibrating creator and when you want something, it can only come to you if you are vibrating on the same wave length as the desired object. Complicated as that sounds what it really means is that to attract something into your space you have to be on the same frequency. How? Pretend, imagine, play act, *be* the desired object.

Let's come back to subconscious mind again for a moment. Remember that it doesn't choose. It can only do what it is told! Here's a case in point. If you pretend you are wealthy by imagining yourself at a fashion house in Paris for the Spring Show—your subconscious won't know it isn't real. It can't discern that. It can only create according to the idea, the blueprint, in your conscious awareness. So ask for what you want. Just align with it, be it, identify with it, live it, embody it, eat, drink, think, speak, and sleep it. Then Bingo, it's on its way.

Okay, so it all sounds like fairytales. You can close the book now if you like, and you'll never know what you missed. I sometimes felt like doing that many years ago but chose to keep practicing. As a result, a beautiful man came into my life, to whom I have already introduced you, along with hosts of other wonders.

A lovely house came into my experience, then later, a much nicer one, and after that, something I was going to say that I had never dreamed of—but that's not true. I certainly had dreamed of it and that's how it came into my ownership.

Through this same process of visualization, I have restored my health. I have achieved a harmonious family relationship, and I have the beautiful and expensive clothes of which I only dreamed when I was shopping at Value Village.

Shall I go on? Yes, I will. For one more marvel.

My car was finally defunct. It seemed no replacement was in sight. So I started *seeing* a lovely little clean car in my head and in my parking spot. I didn't actually name it or see a brand; anything that got me down the road would be better than what I had. It was late April, early May, as I recall, and I kept *seeing* a car. Then on the morning of Mother's Day, my daughter called me. "Mom, don't go anywhere. We are coming over right now." I knew it, and when she arrived—with my new car—I could not feign surprise because right at that moment I "saw" it in my mind's eye. It was a silver VW Beetle!

Once again, I'll get back to vibration and let Esther Hicks, channeling the entities that call themselves

Abraham, say how it works: "Use whatever you can to vibrate in harmony with those things you say you want and when you do, those things that are a vibrational equivalent will flow into your experience in abundance. Not because you deserve it, not because you've earned it, but because it's that natural consequence of The Law of Attraction. "That which is like unto itself is drawn" (excerpted from a workshop in Silver Springs, MD, Saturday, 4/9/97).

Just a line or two ago I said that it's already created. Here's a mind bender looking at you! Remember again about the subconscious mind (which I equate with my Source). *That* is the energy you are using, and when you say it's done, it's done, no two ways about it. So when you are going about your day, with this lovely image of what you have created in your mind's eye, remember to remember that it is already done. Okay, you may not have it in your hand yet, but as you persist in envisioning it, you will. Right here and right now there is immense cause for the deepest gratitude. You who are The Spirit have co-created with your Source, your Origin, something lovely which you have wanted. It is done. Live in ecstatic realization, expectation, and joy.

A few last thoughts. Don't blow it by negating the dream with mental or verbal denials. This can happen so quickly and is usually borne of fear and popular disbelief in the power we each have. The process I have described has worked for me and for the many authors whose works are cited at the end of the book.

Keep your mind on the desired object by writing it down, sticking a picture on the "fridge" or bathroom mirror, and mostly by just enjoying it in your head, and, remember, you have an extraordinary capability here to create what you want to have. It is the expression of your partnership with your Source. Joel Goldsmith has it down to a T in his phrase, "God is the only capacity you have, and therefore there is no limit to your capacity" (from *The Joel Goldsmith Reader*, 1987, pg. 368).

If your job is not quite to your liking, imagine what would improve it and see it done. If there's someone in your life whose behavior troubles you, imagine what you want and see it done. If your income is insufficient, name and imagine what you would like, and see it done (and don't get hung up on how that will come about—that's not your business—that's for Source to figure out).

Please stop here long enough to think about your power to affect the rest of your life or take these ideas into meditation and let them filter in and take hold. People talk of space being the last frontier for humankind to explore—no, it's our fertile mind and the wonder it can envision and accomplish which is the next zone of our exploration.

I will give the final thought and verification to Richard Bach, author of *Illusions,* whose character says on pg. 131, "Richard, you don't have to do anything, you see it done, and it is." And in another place, "To bring a thing into your life, imagine that it is already there."

Chapter Seven

Attract

What you seek is seeking you.
Rumi

You are the attractor of your own experience.
As you look for positive aspects, and make
an effort to find good feeling thoughts
you will hold yourself in a place of positive attraction
and what you want will come faster.
The Law of Attraction, Esther and Jerry Hicks

If I haven't said it before, here it comes again—there's a big mind bender in the offing. "What you think is what you get," and "You'll get what you think about most of the time" (Emerson), and "Like attracts like." And it all comes back to the use of thoughts in your powerful and creative mind.

There is a law at work in the universe which applies continually and consistently, whether you acknowledge and believe it or not, and that system brings to you the essence of whatever you focus your thoughts on most of the time. It is called The Law of Attraction. Mark that phrase: "Whether you acknowledge and believe it or not." Had I learned about that law rather than the catechism in the first grade, I think that my life would have flowed quite differently. No matter, I designed my life before I came to earth and I had some learning to do. My point is that this immutable law is at work all the time in your life, so let's take a good look at it, and then you can make informed choices.

What is The Law of Attraction and how does it operate? According to Marc de Bruin, "The Law of Attraction states that what you consistently think about and have emotion about is what is going to come about" (ezinarticles.com/The-law-of-Attraction).

And why *is* that?

You are pure vibrating energy, and you share that characteristic with all of creation. Rhonda Byrne in her notable book, *The Secret* (www.thesecret.tv), puts it this way: "Everything is energy. You are an energy magnet. So you electrically energize everything to you and electrically energize yourself to everything you want." The reason you are you and not a lobster is due to a difference in vibratory speed, density, and other variables.

Thought is energy. If you *focus* thought on an idea it will take a form—and appear in the physical realm. But there is another very important facet to this creation, and that is *feeling.* If you feel good about the object of your desire, you will attract good results to you. If, on the other hand, you feel unhappy about what you focus on, you will draw a less desirable outcome.

That can be stated another way for greater clarity, and here again, I lean heavily on the ideas of Marc de Bruin.

If you want to attract something lovely and wonderful into your life, but you keep your attention focused on the misery of what you want to remove, you will attract more of the same because that is where your attention and emotions are. If, instead, you really don't want something in your physical experience and center your gaze and love on what you'd like to experience, you will attract that. It is simple. You get what you think about.

Perhaps an example might help elucidate this. You want to move out of your current living situation. First, you need to decide what you don't want. Perhaps the kitchen is too small, perhaps the local transportation is insufficient. Maybe you need more garden space, or a better school district, or would prefer a different housemate. Identifying what you don't want is the beginning of itemizing what you'd prefer.

Next, list what you do want. A bigger kitchen. (Do you want morning sun?) Better bus service? (Outside your door or down the block?) A larger garden? (With a slight slope facing south maybe?) As for the school, should it be smaller, or more rural, or have teachers you know and like? Perhaps you have a housemate in mind—and mind is where it all begins. List the qualities you want to find in that person with all the details. Need I say it, enter into this new plan with love and delight and eagerness because that is part of the creative process.

You know exactly what you want. Now comes the tricky part. Keep *all* of your thoughts on *that* (*on what you want*). You are creating what you are thinking about. At all costs, avoid giving any attention to what you want to leave behind. Don't go there! This is where focus is so important. You will not attract the good things you want into your life by thinking any more about what you don't want. "The only reason that you could ever experience something other than what you desire is because you are giving the majority of your attention to something other than what you desire." Those words are spoken by the authorities on the subject, Esther and Jerry Hicks, in *The Law of Attraction*.

Now let's talk about feelings. How you feel about what you are creating is of paramount importance. When you feel wonderful, happy, and delighted that what you are co-creating with the Universe, it is being magnetized to you. Anticipate your new creation and live emotionally in

56

your new space and exhilarate at waking up there to start every day in your new life.

If you call Auntie Flo and spend an hour reliving memories of the old situation, or talk to your sister and regurgitate the undesirable habits of the housemate from whom you are separating, or give any energy to what you do not want, it will halt the creation of your dream, and possibly replace it.

Remember, you're *always* attracting, *always*. Oh, and one more thing about the new housemate. You have considered the qualities which you would like that person to have. If you will emulate those qualities in yourself and *be* the person you want to live with, not only will you attract such an individual, but you will be in harmony with him or her. Esther and Jerry Hicks in their book, *Getting into the Vortex,* say it this way: "You must become a vibrational match to the qualities you seek because what comes to you always matches you."

What The Law of Attraction spells out is that the quality of your life is in your hands—no one else's. You are the one who creates what you want through correct use of your mind and the empowerment of your emotions. If you are not delightedly happy when you are focused on your creation, then you may not get the result you want. You have to feel good about your desire, and if you are grumping about something that you have been through and didn't enjoy, you are headed for more of the same. If, on the other hand, you keep your thoughts on solutions, on new and wanted directions, and the happy aspects of what is coming to you—your dream will become your reality.

I'd like to add another note about your life being in your hands and no one else's. Perhaps at this point you will ask, "What about the abused baby featured on the news last week?" And "How about the woman who was hit by a truck and paralyzed for life"? Did these people draw in these events and arrange those conditions for themselves?

Yes.

There's another book here, but let me explain briefly how I and many others view this.

You are the expression of Source Energy. You incarnated on to the planet to experience the immense variety which life on earth has to offer. You have had many lifetimes before this one. So did the "baby," though it may look six months old, but it has come with far more wisdom and knowledge than you can know at this point in your evolution. You expected to enjoy life on Earth and knew that the tools outlined above would work for you. You chose your path before you came to the planet so that you could learn and act as the Great Spirit you are. The "baby" understood its path and expected to excel and learn through it. The rendezvous with the truck was also part of her plan to grow for the woman who experienced that.

Looking at life's events in this way whisks those who understand these words out of victimhood and into the driver's seat of their own lives. We have all survived experiences which we could have done without, but many of us, through those very experiences, have built purposeful, happy lives of service and joy.

Remember *who* you are! If you do, your life can flow so much more smoothly.

Please bear in mind that I have but scratched the surface on this subject. I have sought to bring your attention to the existence of this law of the universe and how it will act upon what you think, but the books listed later will take you deeper, and once you really assimilate and practice this, you will wonder why you didn't always know and use it.

Actually you did, but when you came to the planet, so great was the fear around you from generations of struggling humans that your parents and others had also forgotten the gifts they came with. But from here on, the tools are restored to you, and a time will come when everyone will live in this awareness and we shall be at peace in the world.

To set you on what may be a new path for you, I'd like to send you on your way with a powerful thought from *Wells of Abundance* by E.V. Ingraham. "I am filled with the wisdom, love, power and substance of God and as an irresistible magnet I draw to myself all that is needful for my most complete expression of life."

Chapter Eight

Give

The wise man does not lay up treasure.
The more he gives to others the more he has for his own.
Lao Tse

The only way we can get money is by giving it away.
Man was not born to cry.
Joel Goldsmith

There it is in a nutshell. Do I have to tell you what a mind bender *that* is? For most of us, giving first is the wrong way around. We want to see the rent paid, food on the table, and money in the bank before we think of giving anything away. Various sacred texts teach something similar to the following lines from the Bible: "As you give so shall you receive, pressed down, shaken together and running over . . ." (Luke 6:38), which affirms the priority of giving *before* you can expect to receive.

    Can we find any way to sugarcoat such an uncomfortable mandate? It's a toughie, but I can think of a couple.

When we talked earlier about our oneness with all other people, it became clear that we are inextricably connected with all of life. What we do affects all others; the domino effect reverberates across the world; not only that, but what we do to and for others comes back to us in some form or another, partly because it is the law of effect at work, but also because what we do to another, we do to ourselves.

The other thought I have regarding sugarcoating is that when you give, you can *expect* your gift to come back to you multiplied. Who says? It's the testimony of the people for whom wealth and plenty has become a reality.

For centuries, this concept behind generous giving has been called tithing, and though I shall only cite one example here, you can leaf through the Catherine Ponder books listed in the Suggested Reading section and find many, many others whose well-being has been enhanced by their giving. One extraordinary character deserves mention in respect of tithing.

In 1844, John D. Rockefeller tithed $9.50 to the source of his spiritual nourishment. By 1935, his tithes totaled $531,000,000 (from *The Prospering Power of Love* by Catherine Ponder).

Does that make it any easier to give when you are broke and would prefer to buy something for yourself or your family? Maybe not. So why do it? Because you believe that by giving, *you* benefit by that gift. Once again, we are being asked to change a long-ingrained habit of mind, not only to give *before* we get, but also to realize that by giving before we get, we shall ultimately be far better off.

So we come back to thought and you get what you think about and to faith in the process which causes your desire to happen. I'm reminded of the placebo effect—if you think a pill makes a difference then it does. Some smart soul, and I think it was Henry Ford, has said, "If you think you can, or you think you can't, you're right in either case." But there's more to it. We are dealing with belief here, and what one believes happens, and this works both ways, since what you fear you attract.

I started to tithe more than 30 years ago, and initially, it didn't work. Why? As I continued to give, I found that I gave grudgingly. It wasn't that I didn't know the right attitude to have, but I had some mental and emotional blocks, and I just wasn't really getting it. I didn't feel I could afford it. Then I discovered that I was not expecting to be prospered by my tithes (and we shall have more to say on expecting later). Also, I found that my feeling of love and gratitude was absent. So I had to change my thinking, and I started giving gladly, willingly, and happily, knowing that what I gave not only benefited others, but came rushing back to bless me in many ways, and, most important, I gave (and continue to give) with gratitude that I *have it* to give. I know that there is always plenty more coming and the more I give, the more comes. As if that were not enough, I am thrilled that others benefit from what I have to share.

Giving money is essential and wonderful, but there are other ways to give, and again let me remind you that you are giving to yourself because all of us are one. It occurs to me that someone is thinking: What do you mean by that? If we are all one, does that include murderers, rapists, and child molesters? Yes, it does. That is what I mean. There is but One Mind, One Life, One Source, and we are each individual expressions of that Energy. We all have the gifts and the power of The Source—*how we use* them is our unique choice.

So what else might you give to all these other parts of yourself? It takes just an instant of your time to envision the whole world surrounded and immersed in the Love of The Source. This may sound a little woo-woo to some of you, but this is another place where you can create with your visualization, and since thoughts are things, your attention just made the people of the world happier and more prosperous and more aware of their true nature. This is a great gift, because who and what you are impacts everyone, and guess what? All that love comes back to you.

You can give time. You can open a door for another. You can smile at someone you would rather ignore. You can step off the curb to let others pass while inwardly worshipping the true being of each. Namaste! You can do acts of kindness and never tell who did it. You can shut your mouth when you'd rather snap at someone. You can pick up the trash with a kind heart and a blessing for those who left it. You can give in sometimes and not have to get your way. You can listen (have you discovered how much people need an ear?), particularly to the elderly. You can buy coffee for a homeless person. You can share whatever overflows in your material life, whether it be fruit and veggies in the fall, or the willing lend of a tool or a helping hand. Need I go on? You have a fertile mind. The idea is to be free with what you have and share generously. The kinder we are, the sooner we shall have the world peace we all say we want.

What else? Oh yes. You can give total devotion. Whoa! That sounds frightening. I agree and, God knows, I wish I had done that much earlier in life and my earthly passage would have been so much more serene. What does it mean to love unconditionally? It is the ultimate in no-holds-barred giving. It is selfless. It has no ego in it, no sense of what's in it for me. It doesn't expect a return. It seeks only to give love in mountainous quantities and superb quality. And this thought leads me smoothly into the next.

The Golden Rule admonishes us to "Do unto others as you would have them do to you." Have you ever heard of The Platinum Rule? This is quite another ball game.

Once more I return to the story of Roy Harsh whom you have met before in these pages. I was 74; he was 82. I had divorced two years earlier and his wife had died two years earlier. We had known each other slightly over twenty years, but it took no time at all once we became unexpectedly reconnected to know that we would be together to the end and such was Roy's health that we knew that end was not far away.

When I first went to Roy's home, a higgledy-piggledy jungle of possessions collected over sixty years of life in the same dwelling, my eye fell on a tiny brown booklet amidst the chaos on the kitchen table. It was about 4"x 6" and the gold lettering said *The Platinum Rule*. It caught my imagination and I picked it up. Roy explained that it had been written by a friend of his for his family and business associates. "This is the way I want to live," he said. I opened it and began to read.

"You are called to live by the Golden Rule, but you *choose* to live by The Platinum Rule." Then in a few simple, almost stark, words was the primary message: "Do more for others than you would ever expect them to do for you."

I remember wanting to cry and I probably did. What a calling. What a choice. What a way to live a life. I just sat there and looked at Roy marveling that he and I had come together and knew that from now on I would dedicate my time and energy to caring for him through his many maladies with unerring devotion.*

Then I turned the page and read on. "When you adopt The Platinum Rule as a way of life, you will be fulfilled beyond all of your expectations." I recognized this as one of those pivotal moments in life when I was faced with a choice which would entirely change my direction. Here was my opportunity to give unconditional love all the time and in all circumstances. So inwardly I said *yes* that is what I wanted to do no matter what the cost and what I had not ever done heretofore. That decision changed me and brought great opportunities for learning and selflessness.

Roy has since made his transition to the non-physical, but I, in addition to all the other things he taught me, have a road map for the future because as one continues to read that tiny book, the way is spelled out.

What is expected? Do more.
What is the minimum? Do more.
What is required? Do more.
In all your actions, do more.

For family: Do more for your family than you would have them do for you.

For friends: Do more for your friends than you would have them do for you.

For neighbors: Do more for your neighbors than you would have them do for you.

For people I encounter: Do more for people that you encounter than you would have them do for you.

I want and choose to be fulfilled beyond all of my expectations. I want and choose the fullest experience of life that I can possibly have, and I expect to fulfill my highest potential. With that in mind, I practice The Platinum Rule. One day I shall walk on water and through brick walls and manifest the world's best chocolate éclairs in my hand just by thinking about them. Until then, I will love and give with all of my energy.

So I have boiled it down to three areas in which those who are willing to give (and be overwhelmingly blessed for it) can proceed, and in doing so, further their own evolution and that of all living things. Give of your income and substance, give of your time and love, and then give everything—everything—and allow your Source to sustain your life, as you have sought it to gift others.

*I don't know whether the *The Platinum Rule*—in the form outlined above—was ever published. I think not. Its authors, Richard Altig and Ilija Orlovic, wrote it for Richard's friends, family, and business associates.

Chapter Nine
Be Grateful

If the only prayer you ever said in your whole life was "Thank you," it would suffice.
Meister Eckhart

Once you are grateful you are in an energy that creates miracles.
The Attractor Factor, Dr. Joe Vitale

There is a consistent idea which runs through this book and it has been the overpowering importance of thought. Now, as we consider the subject of gratitude, we shall get a refresher on thinking thoughts and how best to handle them.

When I was a child, one of the first literary giants of whom I ever heard and whose work I grew to love, was G. K. Chesterton. He, too, was born in Sussex, England, and his stories, plays, and poems reflect his inquiring mind and humor and love of the Chalk Downs and the proximity of the English Channel. For all my familiarity with his work, it was not until recently–like yesterday–that I discovered his thoughts on gratitude. He says, "I would maintain that thanks are the highest form of thought and that gratitude is happiness doubled by wonder."

That makes me shiver. First, because it takes me back to an association formed in childhood, and second, because I so firmly believe that he is right. Clearly, gratitude is a function of thought and the power of thought, and the extraordinary functions of mind are, I believe, the last frontier for our fervent exploration and the doorway to total freedom.

How do I arrive at that? It's not rocket science! I look around me. I read history and I observe that a relatively small and rather hairless animal has outsmarted larger creatures, and because it carries a box in its apex which can analyze, evaluate, and choose, it has changed the landscape on the planet immeasurably in my lifetime. It has done that because of this awesome ability to take an idea and create something of value to billions of its kind. That awesome ability is thought.

We have found that thought—though suspended in meditation—precedes choice, underlies visualization, investigates worthiness, guides speech, clarifies oneness with all creation, validates giving, and attracts good.   As you read on you will find that thought also justifies our expectations, informs our actions, and facilitates the ultimate act of surrender. What an awesome and glorious gift we have been given. Let us consider now how it can contribute to our well-being as gratitude.

Do you want to be liked and loved? I have a feeling that the answer will be, "Yes, of course I do. Don't we all want that?" Then if you are grateful when you receive a gift, you are well on your way to great popularity. You have experienced the happiness you feel when someone is ecstatic about your present to them. That lovely warm fuzzy fills you in a way that *getting* gifts can't. Expressing gratitude, besides being a cultural nicety, carries a lovable charm with it. The poet Rumi captured this idea when he wrote, "Gratitude is the most exquisite form of courtesy."

That is what you experience on the human level, but when you are grateful to The Universe for the good that comes to you, it seems to open the floodgates to rain more wonders down upon you. Why would that be? We have talked about the Law of Attraction and how one good thought invites another, and another, and another until a time comes when you can only attract the best into your life experience. Not only that, but the act of gratitude expands your awareness of the overflowing goodness of everything around you, and the more you see to be grateful for, the more beautiful happenings and people and circumstances crowd into your life. And then—as if that were not enough—you get happier and happier, and, after all, isn't that what life and all our efforts are about? Does it get any better than that? According to Dr. Joe Vitale, it does, because in his book, *The Attractor Factor*, he says, "Once you are grateful, you are in an energy that creates miracles."

Just in case you think it's all been said and we've covered the ground, let's examine another way in which being grateful blesses you.

You know how your mind is always all over the place? You know how it jumps from one thing to another without so much as a please or thank you and very often stirs up trouble for you by churning up negative thoughts and reminding you what a klutz you are when it (your mind) isn't running things?

Well here's the antidote which will rein in your capricious thinking. When your thoughts are focused on being grateful for all the wonders you keep on receiving, there is no avenue through which the mind can enter and claim your attention, or divert it into worry or criticism or preoccupations which cause more of the same. It's a win-win situation, and, for me, it's the happiest possible use of my time and faculties.

Oh, and another thing about gratitude. I don't pray anymore. I haven't prayed for years. But when there is something that I want, I claim it. I am one with my Source. Source lacks nothing, so neither do I. I simply name the item and say, "Thank You," and I don't stop saying that until the dream is realized. Does that sound bombastic? Or does it sound like using The Law of Attraction?

Just in case you're wondering how being grateful is going to make you wealthier and more prosperous, consider this: If you are busy being happy and grateful for all the good stuff and getting happier all the time, you are also going to be successful in whatever you do because "You are not happy because you are successful; you are successful because you are happy," said The Buddha.

Gratitude is a habit of mind. Once you start doing it, you just keep on it doing because it feels so good. Personally, I find that the very best way to get what I want is to speak aloud the desire of my heart and then say, "Thank You" right then before it shows up. It works like a charm.

I have another ploy which I have come to trust and practice. I write a daily Gratitude List, and this idea came out of my reading the books of Esther and Jerry Hicks. I sit at my desk first thing in the morning and write, "I am grateful for . . ." and fill a page. I find this practice not only keeps me on track, but it causes me to have a greater awareness of the gifts of sight, sound, and touch which come throughout the day so that nothing interrupts my thankfulness for everything.

Chapter Ten

Expect

Expect everything then
nothing comes unexpected.
Norton Juster, The Phantom Tollbooth

I feel a very short segment in the making, mostly because I have no idea what I am talking about and am full of questions, except when I deal with Source. Then I definitely know what to expect.

Webster says expectation is "anticipation of a future good." I wonder sometimes whether popular understanding and usage don't fall far from the mark here because I have noticed that my expectations can get me into a heap of trouble.

We tend to want other people to fulfill our expectations, and, yes, that is anticipation of a future good, but is it realistic for us to pin our hopes on what others may or not choose to deliver? But, of course, you could argue that that would depend upon where we stand in their lives and what our expectations might be.

We cannot affirm for other people, and yet we commonly expect our children to do well in school and life. We often assume a certain behavior from a spouse or partner. We expect the contractor to fulfill his promise. We rely on laws being applied universally. We anticipate that others will be honest—even though we may not be. And not only do we expect others do to thus and so, how often do we fall short in the expectations of others—and of ourselves?

Are we on safe ground in presuming certain performances? We go on vacation expecting to have a good time, but so many variables enter in which can effect that expectation—not to mention that we are told to expect the unexpected, and that often happens when we least expect it. And again, we are admonished to expect change which is probably the most certain thing in our experience. We plant a shrub or put seeds into the ground reckoning on their growth, yet how much control do we really have of that, or anything else?

"Expect the best" we're told, but do we really control that occurrence? How and when is it reasonable to expect the best? And yet, how can we not expect the best when we have set our minds to accomplish something and in expecting the best, we are proclaiming our own positive attitude? After all, if I decide that I want a particular item and I think about it, visualize it, claim it, and am grateful for it before it shows up in my experience, am I not entitled to expect it?

It seems to me that the only life from which I may reasonably expect anything is my own. Everyone else's is none of my business and that includes spouses and children. So perhaps we can agree that we do mess with the lives of others, but should put the focus on our own.

We select an object or a condition, and we set the wheels in motion for its attainment. That means acceptance, definition, refinement, visualization, gratitude, belief, *and* expectation. We expect the Universe to deliver, and it does every time according to our belief. You can look at expectation as a magnet, because it is thought in action.

Do you want your children to do well in school and life? Don't we all want that? You can and doubtless will expect wonderful outcomes. But instead of nagging the hell out of them, *visualize* their success. Thought is the way to create, not constant verbal reminders. Yes, you can throw in incentives, but then leave the matter alone. Let them be themselves and, with your loving encouragement and care, allow them to develop who they are. They came in with a life plan, and excelling in school may not be part of that, and becoming an aeronautical engineer may not be their goal, but with your unconditional love and acceptance, rather than egoistic expectations, you may find that you have a world-class concert pianist on your hands or a spirit who is here to solve the world energy crises and came through you to accomplish this—they will not have to do it in spite of you. The most constructive thing you can do for your children might be to bear in mind the follow words from *Getting into the Vortex* by Esther and Jerry Hicks: "All people in your life will consistently give you what you expect."

The strength of expecting lies in *your* thinking, not in anyone else's doing. It's all in your attitude. The only person you can truly expect for or of is yourself and the reason for that is that if you are plugged into your Real Self, what you affirm will happen. For me, anyway, the only thing that I can expect and depend on is that Source will deliver according to my use of the universal laws of life. In other words, "You get what you think."

So go for it. Expect the marvelous things that you have set in motion to occur, and if you want the same for others, visualize "This or something better."

Perhaps the best way to use expectation in regard to other people is to expect or "see" them fulfilling their own unique fullest potential, whatever that happens to be, rather than pressuring them to fulfill your own selfish fulfillment needs, which might well be called a toxic expectation, and deserves to be expectorated!

So my message to myself is, "I expect the very best from The Source in accordance with my use of my creative thinking. I expect to feel well and have a strong sense of well-being. I expect to have loving friends and attract them with love. I expect to live in abundance, and I expect to fulfill the purpose for which I came to the planet." In terms of other people, "I expect them to develop their own unique magnificence, whether or not I understand their journey and actions, and I send them on their way with my unconditional love, support, and reverence."

Chapter Eleven

Act

A Journey of a thousand leagues begins with a single step.
Confucius

Do what you can from where you are with what you've got.
Infinite Possibilities, Mike Dooley

This is where it all comes together. You have covered so much ground and been exposed to many different ways of thinking and now is the time to integrate all the information and take action to achieve your dreams. And that may sound strange because there is a sense in which it's all been a forward action, it's all been a gathering of material to arrive at this desired place.

There are several important points which I want to emphasize in this segment.

First on the agenda is *Listen!* You have done so much work thinking about how to choose and attract, change attitudes and expectations, and be open to your True Self. Now ask yourself to become more deeply and constantly aware of your feelings and wants and go deeper into that meditative state from which comes much clarity.

When you stir at midnight or in the pale gray light of dawn, ideas will come and present themselves. They may clamor for attention or just drift through your consciousness, and whichever way they come—take notice. You have asked to be guided, you have done all of the "homework" in the previous pages, and now your inner voices are communicating with you and directing you. Take notice. Listen.

I have found it desirable—even necessary—to have a pen and paper handy in the car, by my bed, in the office, and in the kitchen to jot down these ideas before they evaporate. I know that sounds dramatic, but haven't you had the experience of a flash of genius in the dark of night which *of course* you'll remember— and it's gone by daybreak? I emphasize this because some ideas which come to you may seem totally outlandish, impossible, or ridiculous, but for every invention out there which was mind-boggling when it first appeared but now is commonplace, someone had a weird hunch and ran
with it.

Remember the title of the song by Eddie Watkins, Jr., "You are the Place Where God Shows Up," which is on his CD called *When you Believe*? You are a receptacle of all intelligence, all information, all wisdom, and all know-how, because you are the expression of The Source. So maybe, just maybe, you'll want to listen, take note of the ideas, and then spring into action. That's a good start, but not quite enough because to get where you want to go you will have to stay with it. Mike Dooley, in his books, writes of what is needed here, and of what he himself and all successful people have done: "Take some action. Consistent action is of paramount importance. Again it's not so much because of what we might receive, but how we put ourselves in the position of receivership of life's magic (*Infinite Possibilities*)."

This can be scary (and we'll talk more of that in Twelve and a Half) but, for now, go for it fearlessly—trust the process.

A second point I'd like to emphasize is *haste*. Whatever it is that you are prompted to do—do it now. Don't delay. Process what has to be done and get with it immediately. If you don't, it can easily slip away, or, before you know it, someone else who also had a neat idea is working on it and reaping the profits of which you dreamed. I am not saying that there aren't enough space and ideas for everyone, but there is what Carl Jung called The Collective Consciousness, and it's kind of a soup of all ideas for everyone to dip into. So if another acts on "your" idea before you do, you may be able to tweak it a bit, or package it differently and still run with it. But I say it again, "Strike while the iron is hot" and get on with whatever you are going to do *now*. Also, try to avoid second guessing yourself; try to avoid questioning, just explore the idea thoroughly and then make it happen. Sometimes we think it can wait, or we are not quite ready, or we must "clear our decks" first. Let's hear what David J. Schwartz has to offer on this subject in his book, *The Magic of Thinking Big*: "Don't wait until conditions are perfect. They never will be. Expect future obstacles and difficulties and solve them as they arise." And, in another place, the same author writes, "Don't wait for the spirit to move you, take action, dig in and you'll move toward spirit."

One more thing I want to restate before I make my final point. *Trust yourself.* Bear in mind as you do that you are one with your soul, your Life-Force—that which lives in you. We have the tendency to think that we have a life and that "God" is helping us in it. In my thinking, The Spirit is the life of you, and if you will allow it that Energy can do unbelievable things through you. Someone has said that "We are not humans on a spiritual path; we are spirits on a human path." So when I suggest that you trust yourself, I am indicating that you might trust Your Self—that which lives you—and be amazed at the outcome. "Within you now lies the power to do things you had never dreamed of and this power becomes available to you as soon as you change your beliefs." That's Thomas Edison's view on the matter, and he probably knew a thing or two.

Now listen up and get this. As you go about doing what has to be done in the accomplishment of your dreams, act as if they were already an accomplished fact.

Again—please take this in, it is *so* essential. The Law of Attraction requires that you embody, identify with, and live in and with what you have claimed as yours. If it's more money you are working toward, live as if you had it. That doesn't mean spend beyond your current resources, but you can window or catalog shop and imagine you have what you see and feel the delight. Fill your mind and senses with the abundance you are seeking, and love it. If it's a car you are after, spend some mental time driving it down the road and feeling the exhilaration. If wonderful health is your desire, evict all thought of illness and feel the freedom of wellness.

To the degree that you embody the gifts you seek, to the extent that you vibrate in harmony with what you want to manifest—all will be drawn irresistibly to you and show up in your material experience. And just for an extra impetus—be grateful for it. Your desire is already created in The Universal Mind so now is the time for utter delight. Knowing without a whiff of doubt that you already *have* what you desire is the strongest attractor you can emit.

Chapter Twelve

Release

*For whatever you want, rid yourself of the conception
of how you'll get it.*
Infinite Possibilities, Mike Dooley

You're almost there. You know how to quiet your mind
and direct creative choices. You understand
unworthiness and its pitfalls and have learned to use
your voice in attainment of your desires. You've
discovered what your imagination can do and the
wealth in giving and in forgiving. You're acquainted with
the benefits of gratitude, and inevitability of attracting
according to your thoughts and vibration.

Now we approach the final step—which is the
mother of all mind benders.

At this point you may well be asking yourself,
"How am I going to make all his happen? The simple
answer is, *you* don't *make* anything happen. It's none of
your business. In our "normal" world of planning and
activity, how to accomplish a goal would be a high

priority, but you've elected to go another route with the kind of thinking and approach which we have explored together. In this realm, you will let the Source accomplish what you desire. I'll restate that so that you can be sure that you read it correctly. The Source does it for you! By following the steps outlined, you have done your part. Rest with that. All *you* have to do now is *let go* and detach from all outcomes.

Let go. It's so simple. Let go. Two little, teeny-tiny words—but what do they really involve?

Those words mean that it's not up to you to make anything happen, as previously stated. You've done your part. You've connected with your True Self, made a claim, thunk a thought, imagined, visualized, loved universally and forgiven, displaced possible obstacles, expressed gratitude and *accepted,* and acted upon your desired good. Take a deep breath. You're done but for possibly the most vital step of all. *Release.* Get out of your own way. *Allow* events to unfold, trust the process, and reject any more rational thought on the subject.

The how and the when is out of your hands.

But why? The question immediately arises. And the answer is because Source is the only one with all the answers. Because only Source knows all facets of your life and all lives which will be affected in a way that you cannot begin to comprehend. What happens with you and through you is affected by and affects all other beings on earth.

Do I recall having once heard that if a butterfly folds its wings in Seattle its action reverberates in Tokyo?

We are co-creators with The Infinite and our power comes from union with that Power.

Eckhart Tolle has a thought on this: "Surrender is the simple but profound wisdom of yielding to, rather than opposing the flow of life" (from the book *The Power of Now* by Eckhart Tolle reprinted with permission of New World Library, Novato, CA, www.thenewworldlibrary.com).

You Are in Charge of Your Thought but Not Outcomes

We tend to think that we are in charge, but anyone who has experienced the sudden death of a loved one, or the loss of a faculty, will know that there is a power beyond our scope which moves in awesome and mysterious ways to accomplish the best for all of us.

But since you are so action-oriented, there are actually some things you *can* do to hasten the accomplishment of your dreams.

First, you can banish all thoughts on the subject from your mind. As an old friend of mine would say, "If you dig up the corn to see if it's growing, you may stunt or possibly kill it."

Second, you can give no energy at all to considering how the result of your efforts might appear.

Third, you can go out into the sunlight or the snow and have fun and be ecstatically happy that your desires are already fulfilled in the Mind of the Infinite and that all you have to do is expect their arrival with unbounded joy.

Fourth—and above all else—you can obliterate worry! Remember, if you worry, you are entertaining an opposing thought which will create something you don't want.

Fifth, you can remind yourself that "This or something better" is on its way to you.

Until we really realize that we *are* the creative energy of Source, there is a tendency to think small, limited, and confined, but the Great Energy conceives of only the biggest, best, and most wonderful, so It may process your request with a largess you cannot imagine.

It has happened to me, and at the risk of repeating myself, I will explain.

After many unsettling years during which I studied assiduously how to attract what I wanted into my life, I told the Universe that I want to be in love again. Not too long after that I asked for a companion to take me to the opera and theatre. Time passed. I didn't give it much thought. I knew it was done. But I bought clothes, I spruced up my appearance, I listened to beautiful music, I anticipated the coming joy while living happily in the present moment.

Then, one day I met a man with whom I had been slightly acquainted for twenty odd years. Within two weeks, I was totally in love and the glory of it was that not only was I in love as never before, but he was passionate about opera and ballet and music, and we went and loved it together.

That's what I meant when I said you never know what The Universe has in mind when you make your claim upon it and then surrender to the flow of life. Dare to think big. Stretch yourself into extravagant thinking. Know that you can have what you want. Then forget trying to make it happen. Let it go.

I told you it was simple All it takes is mind control. I don't really mean to be flip about this. I know the struggles it can involve to let go and stay clear of the subject. You can do it. Go out and play. Learn how to throw the javelin. Join a gardening club. Learn Chinese. Go dancing. Take a trip to Lhasa, anything to get your mind occupied, and do so with the absolute certainty that what you have claimed of the Source, It will deliver when the time is right. Source wants you to be fulfilled and happy. It is expressing Itself as you. You are the focus of Its love, and It wants to give to you everything you want. Let It.

I'll close with an inspiring poem by Richard Wilbur, which while utterly lyrical, steers us into contemplating the effects of allowing life to flow. I hope that it will also remind you that what you have asked for will have effects more far reaching than you can imagine. It is called *Two Voices in a Field, The Milkweed Speaks . . ."* and comes from the Spoken Arts Poetry Collection, Vol. 3, Disc, 2. (If you are not familiar with the milkweed plant, or any plant which spills its seed to the wind for dispersal, just consider the for-get-me-not or dandelion—the effect and the proliferation are the same.)

"White seeds are flying out of my burst pod.
What power had I before I learned to yield?
Shatter me Great Wind—I shall possess the field."

Chapter Twelve and a Quarter
Tools

We shall neither fail nor falter we shall not weaken or tire . . .
give us the tools and we shall finish the job.
Winston Churchill

Tut, tut, tut . . .

If you are peaking at this point before you've read the whole text—don't. Quit now! What follows in this brief segment will then make much more sense.

Forty years ago, I attended several of John Boyle's Omega Seminars. After four intensive days of what was then mind blowing material which held the potential to change lives, John delivered a concluding message which I have never forgotten and will attempt to paraphrase.

You have been given, he would say, some valuable tools. You can take them away with you and use them daily and thereby grow wealthy, happy, and wise, or you can put them in the tool chest (tucked away somewhere at the back of your mind) and think you'll remember what you have just learned.

This, John said, was what so many people do. They study new material with good intentions; they want to grow. That's why they came to the seminar in the first place, but they think they'll never forget the experience and never stop practicing what they learned.

I was one of those.

It doesn't work that way. If you want to play pro tennis, you're out on the court 6-8-10 hours a day.

If you want to be a concert violinist, you practice long after everyone else has gone home. If you want to be an Olympic gymnast, you will welcome a punishing routine, and if you choose to change your mind, your ideas, your habits, and the quality of your life, you will keep this little book close by, refer to it until it becomes second-nature, and see the changes happen. As I have said, I didn't follow the advice—I knew it all—so my evolution took much longer.

So, here you are. It's your lovely life. You are the only one who can do it for you.

What choice will you make?

Chapter Twelve and a Half
Self-Doubt

Doubt is a pain too lonely to know
that faith is its twin
Kahlil Gibran

It's likely that you will go merrily along with all this for a few exuberant days or weeks, then after a fervent and spirited beginning, something changes. You feel out of sorts, you have a fender bender, the cat gets lost, or there's an argument . . . . Suddenly you are not your "normal" self. Everything seems to go to the dogs; suddenly you are afraid and out of your comfort zone. And you think, "What's the use? Why bother? Nothing works." You are discouraged.

Good! It's working.

I warned you that your mind wouldn't cooperate. So join the club of all those who have gone before and hauled themselves into recovery and refused to give up. Self-doubt is a common reaction, probably inevitable, and certainly not the end of your efforts.

Change your self-talk to "I can do this." "This stuff works." "I'm right on target." "I'm in exactly the right place." Boost your own morale here and keep moving forward. As you chalk up the winnings, you'll be so glad.

What has happened is that you have reached what Bob Proctor and Michelle Blood call "The Terror Barrier." Your ego is throwing a tantrum because you are bent on change and will not allow your rapacious mind to lead you around by the nose and halt your progress toward greater awareness.

In their book, *Be a Magnet to Money,* these authors suggest, "Just do it, even if you do it scared." It all looks like a useless endeavor and you might as well give up. You are experiencing what Bob and Michelle call F.E.A.R. (False Evidence Appearing Real).

The jolt to your system offered by the upset you've experienced is just a ploy that the mind uses to deflect your purpose. That's why I call it "good." If the new approach wasn't a threat and wasn't working, your mind wouldn't throw a tizzy-fit.

Just in case you think you the only one who has faced self-concept issues, I know about those. Even now, I sometimes look in the mirror and think, What the hell do you think you are doing? Go home and weed the garden. Then I think, No, I *will* do this. I *can* do this. I am able, and I think with D.J. Schwarz who writes in *Think Big*, "Action cures fear." I have all that it takes within me. Then I just get on with it—and do it anyway. We're gonna get these attacks from time to time. Put on a smile and say, "I feel better" and get going.

Twelve and Three Quarters

Perpetual Joy

Joy is a net of love by which you can catch souls.
A joyful heart is the inevitable result of a heart
brimming with love.
Mother Teresa

Wow! Perpetual that means always, consistent, continual. Is that possible? Can one live in joy all the time? Perhaps you can't pull that off yet. Neither can I, but I practice it continually, and one day I believe that I shall get there.

So what is joy and why is it important? I have a definition which works for me, but before I share it, let's hear what some others have to offer.

"Joy does not come from what you do; it flows into what you do, and into the world from deep within you" (*A New Earth*, Eckhart Tolle).

"I slept and dreamt that life was joy. I woke and saw that life was service. I acted and behold service was joy" (Rabindranath Tagore).

"Total joy does not come from riches, or from the praise of men, but from doing something worthwhile"(Sir Wilfred Grenfell).

"Joy is not in things, it is in us" (Richard Wagner).

These are a few voices with insightful words about joy—and of course there are many more. What I have arrived at has taken many years to evolve, and I have found that when I am in a state of joy it is because I have surrendered (again) to the Life within, and while making my plans and setting them in motion and visualizing all the goodies I want, I can take a deep breath—let go and allow that which lives me to take over.

This practice is most effective and most difficult when things in my life are challenging; when I want more, or less, of something; when I am off balance and overwhelmed. For it is just then, in those moments, that it is most necessary to release everything. It is then that I find joy. It is in the over-riding conviction that Source Energy is—with my co-creativity—handling everything and no more input or concern from me is desirable.

I don't live in joy because everything is going well in my life. Everything is going well I my life because I life in joy. And that's a choice because there are times when I feel like weeping because things haven't gone according to what I thought was the plan.

A case in point occurred after completing this book. My work ended with this very segment and the next day I went to the Department of Licensing to renew my driver's license—and I could not see the letters in the monitor! Think about that. The kindly clerk gave me a form to take with me. "Have your ophthalmologist fill this out," she said.

A gloom fell upon me. "Be still" said that ever-present inner voice, "and know that I am God" (Psalms 46:10). But another voice—mine—was shrieking, "This is the end of life as I know it." Then the former voice again over the panicked clamor: "You are okay. Life is unfolding differently than you had expected and is always ecstatically lovely if you will allow it to unfold." Somewhere in the unsettled chaos, Mike Dooley's words came in too: "You are unlimited beyond your wildest imaginings."

I've been through all kinds of switchbacks and mind benders in my life, and I want to be totally open to whatever comes and use it as fuel for joy. Then I think of the words of Abraham: "You are joy looking for a way to express. It's not just that your purpose is joy; it is that you *are* joy. You are love and joy and freedom and clarity expressing" (Esther and Jerry Hicks).

My life is an expression of Source energy, and Source is joy. In the moments when fear or pain or hesitation come near I want to have only one answer to the question posed by the Sufi mystic, Pah Vilayer Khan, who asks, "Why aren't you dancing for joy at this very moment?" And my response is, "I will, and I am because I know that everything is just as it should be and is perfect."

Several days passed before I got the reassurance that my eyes were okay, and my ophthalmologist cleared me to continue driving. I understand the whole incident better now. The Source was giving me the opportunity to surrender my life and allow events to unfold while I maintained my joy. By the time I actually renewed my license, I felt total joy no matter what the outcome. I do have a driver's license now.

Conclusion

*Whatever you have accomplished up until now
is a small fraction of what is truly possible for you.*
Brian Tracy* (see Suggested Reading)

You are unlimited beyond your wildest imaginings.
Infinite Possibilities, Mike Dooley

I've tried to create a simple way for you to get from where you are to where you would like to be, and I, had I known all this years ago, would also be there by now.

And just look at what a flight of steps you've mounted. You've doubtless had to stop and take a breath from time to time and pause to evaluate the mind benders along the way, and perhaps have found that

If you think, you are choosing.
If you visualize you are thinking, choosing, and attracting.

If you are grateful, you can certainly expect, and if you are attracting wonderful things, you are happy.

If you are happy, you are attracting even more happiness and with happiness comes success.

If you speak positively, you are thinking; if you are visualizing, you are ecstatic and grateful; and if you are grateful, you are attracting.

If you are wanting good things for others, you are forgiving and appreciating, and if you are accepting and acting, you are on target for fulfillment.

If you've hauled yourself beyond self-doubt, and are using the tools, it's a no-brainer, *and* if you are doing all of this, you are going to be filled with joy, *not* because you have a cartload of cool stuff, but because you have learned how to let the Spirit work with and through you and have broken out of your limitations into a blissful and serene space.

You have also found that I have repeated myself mercilessly. Says Richard Bach, author of *Illusions,* "teaching is reminding others of what they know just as well as you," and, in another place, "You teach best when you most need to learn."

Congratulations for having come to the end of the book. These steps have brought me from pain and penury to peace and plenty, and they are certainly not all that can be said. The books listed in Suggested Reading will inform you further. It is my visualization, my thinking, my knowing, and my deepest desire that what you have found in these pages will spur you on to experience the boundless abundance of life through the use of your unlimited creative power.

If you were to take away *one* thing above all else from this book, I hope it will be the conviction that you have no limits, that you "can do," that you are the creator of your life's experience, and that anything is possible.

Ok, I lied, there are four—but I want them all for you, Namaste!

Index

Suggested Reading

Adington, Jack, *Fifteen Keys to Prosperity,* Abundant Living Foundation

Allen, James, *As a Man Thinketh,* The Peter Pauper Press

Anthony, Dr. Robert, *Beyond Positive Thinking,* Morgan & James, New York

Behrend, Genevieve, *Attaining Your Desires,* Bottom of the Hill Publishing

Bales, Frederick. *Hidden Power for Human Problems,* Prentice Hall Inc.

Bryrne, Rhonda, *The Secret,* Atria Books

Dooley, Mike, *Infinite Possibilities,* Atria Press, www.Tut.com

_____, *Notes from the Universe,* Atria Press

Dyer, Dr. Wayne, *You'll See it When You believe It,* Quill

_____, *The power of Intention,* Hay House

Gawain, Shakti, Creative *Visualization,* Bantam, New York

Goldsmith, Joel, *Invisible Supply,* Harper, San Francisco

_____, *Man Was Not Born To Cry*

Haanel, Charles E., *The Master Key System,* Penguin

Hicks, Esther and Jerry, *The Astonishing Power of Emotions*

_____, *Ask and it is Given*

_____, *Money and the Law of Attraction*

www.AbrahamHicks.com, Phone: 830-755-2299

Ingraham, E.V., *Wells of Abundance,* Devorss & Co.

Yearling Mulford, Prentice, *Thoughts Are Things,* Health Research

Myss, Carolyn, *Why People Don't Heal and How They Can,* Three Rivers Press, New York

Murphy, Joseph, D.D., D.R.S., Ph.D., L.L., *Your Infinite Power to be Rich*

Ponder, Catherine, *The Dynamic laws of Prosperity,* Devorss & Co.

_____, *Open Your Mind to Prosperity,* Devorss & Co.

_____, *The Prospering Power of Love*

Proctor, Bob and Michelle Blood, *Be a Magnet to Money*, Price, John Randolph, *The Abundance Book,* Hay House Inc.

_____, *Living a Life of Joy,* Fawcett, Columbine

_____, *Nothing Is Too Good To Be True,* Hay House

Schwartz, D.L., *Thinking Big,* Pocket Books

Tracy, Brian,

Weed, Joseph L., *Wisdom of the Mystic Masters,* Reward Books

Websites:

*www.briantracy.com. Brian Tracy is chairman and CEO of Brian Tracy International, a company specializing in the training and development of individuals and organizations.

www.twelveandthreequartersteps.com